Families

by Margie Burton, Cathy French, and Tammy Jones

There are many kinds of families.
Some families are small.

Some families are big.

Some families live together.
Some families do not.

Some children live
with their moms.

Some live with their dads.

Some live with
their grandparents.

Some live
with someone else.

Some families do not have children.

There are many kinds of families.

Many families have homes.
This family lives in a house
on a farm.

This family lives in an apartment
in the city.

Families give us food to eat.

Families give us clothes to wear.

Families give us love. They
take care of us when
we are sick.

They take us to the park to play and have fun.

Families work together.

They help each other.

Families learn together.
They learn from each other.

Families have rules. Rules help
keep families safe.

Rules help my sister and me
get along with each other.

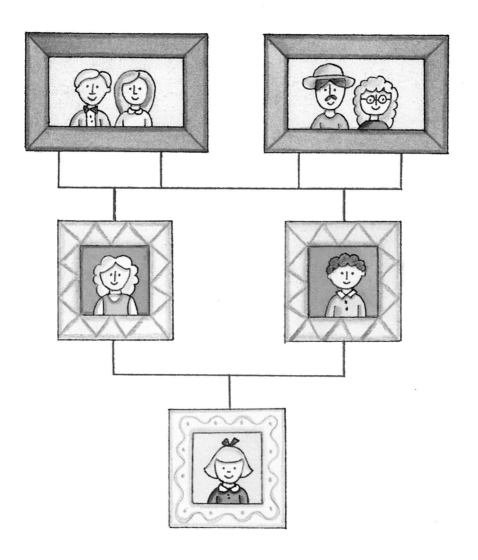

The people who love you and take care
of you are your family.